We Go to the ZOO

by Cindy Kane

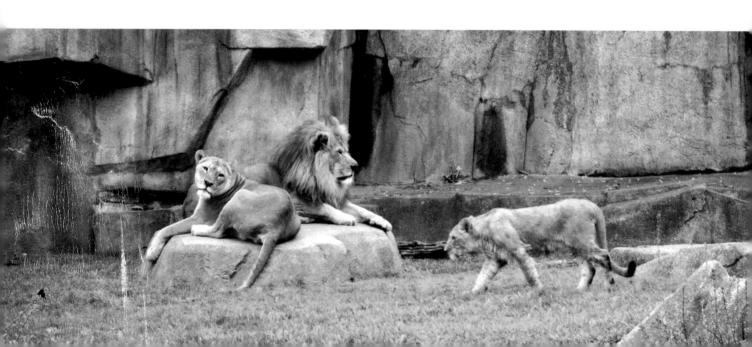

We go to the zoo.

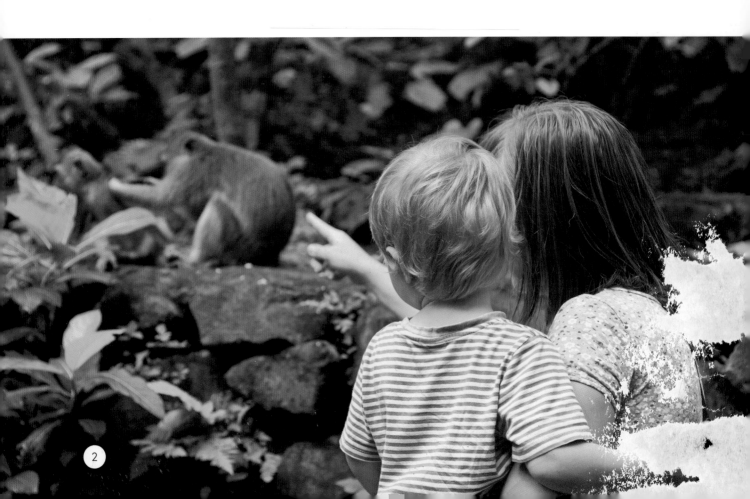

We see the bats.

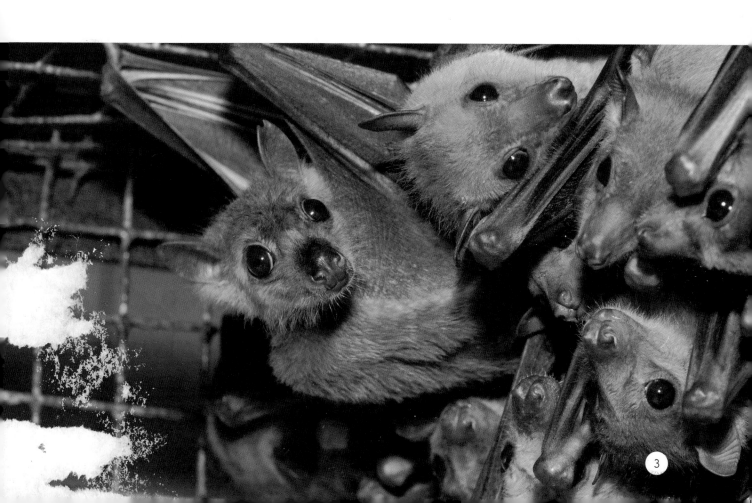

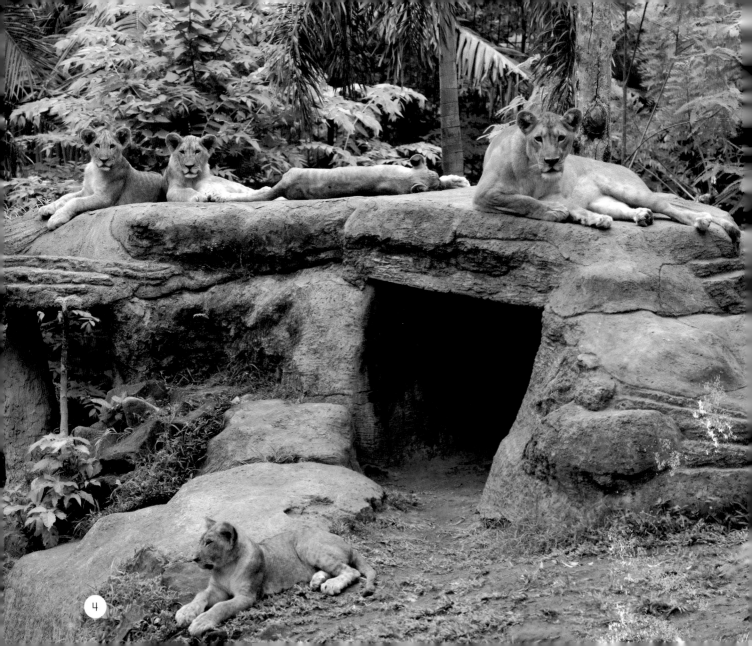

We see the big cats.

We see the birds.

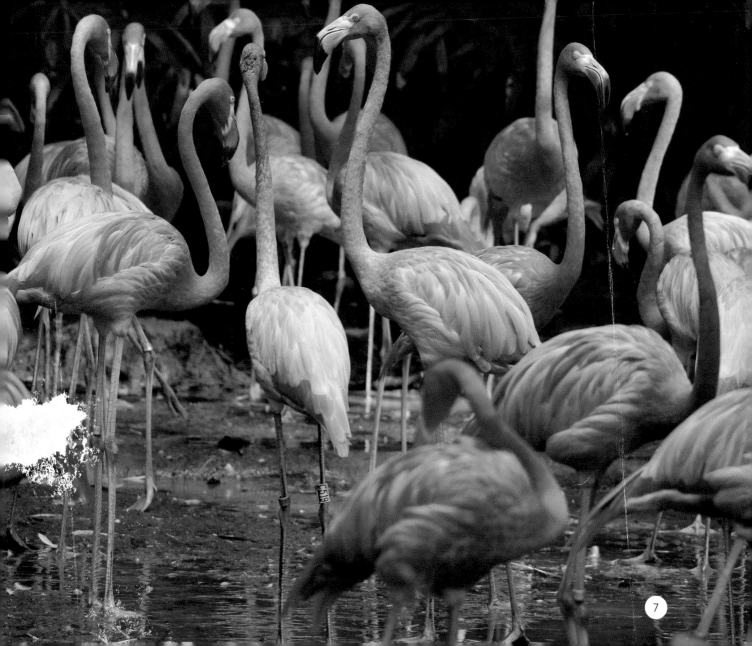

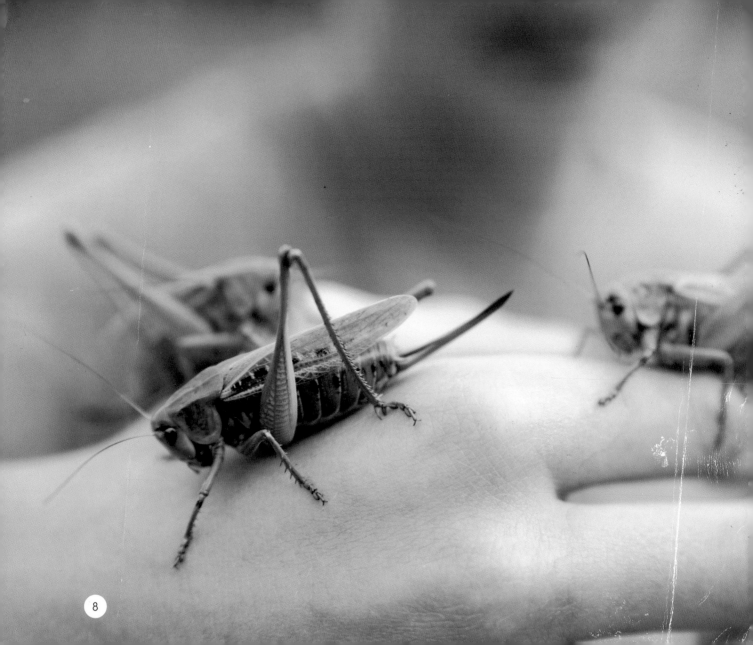

We see the bugs.

We see the fish.

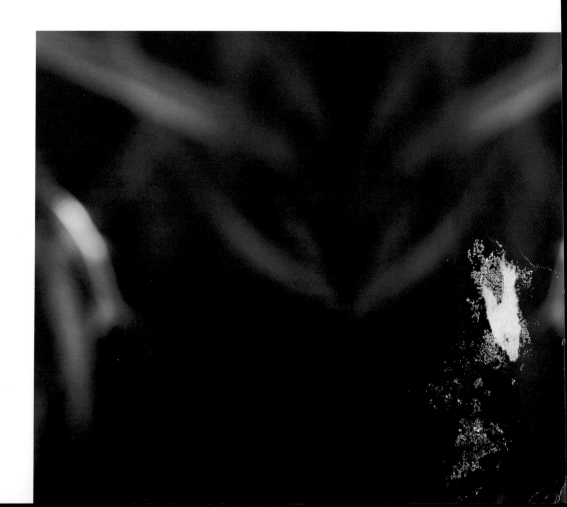

We see fins on the fish.

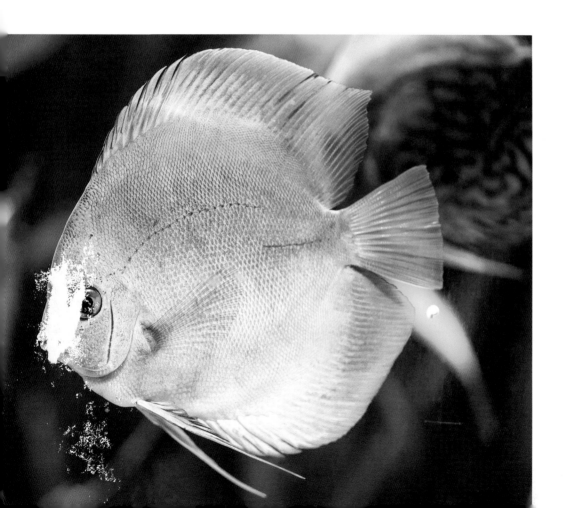

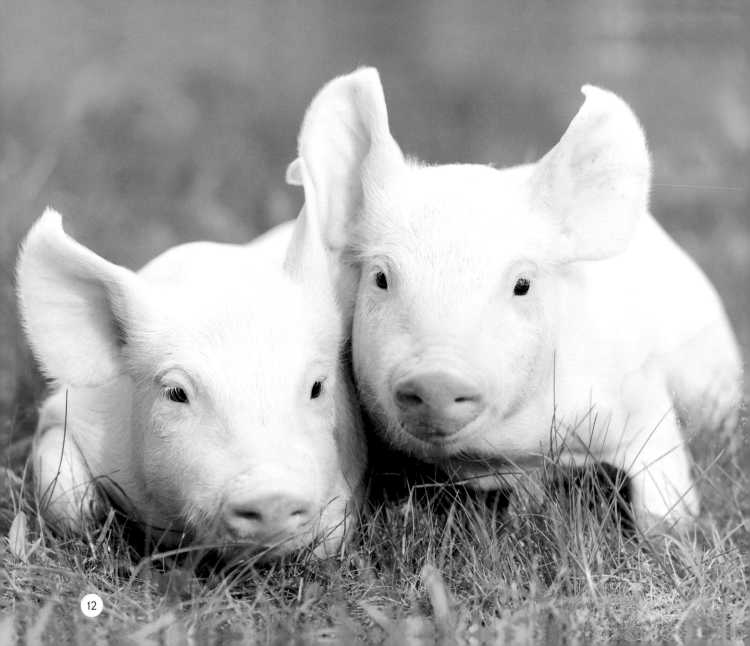

We see the pigs.

We see the hens.

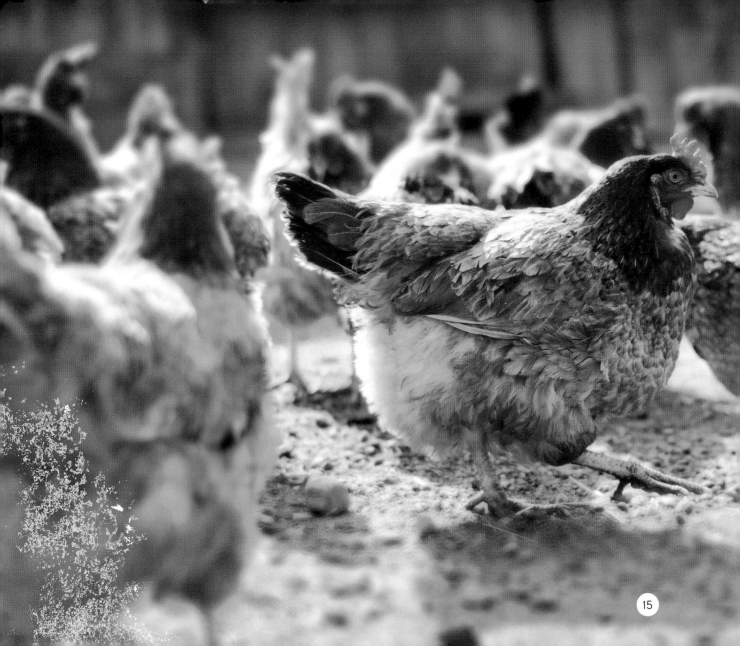

We have fun at the zoo.

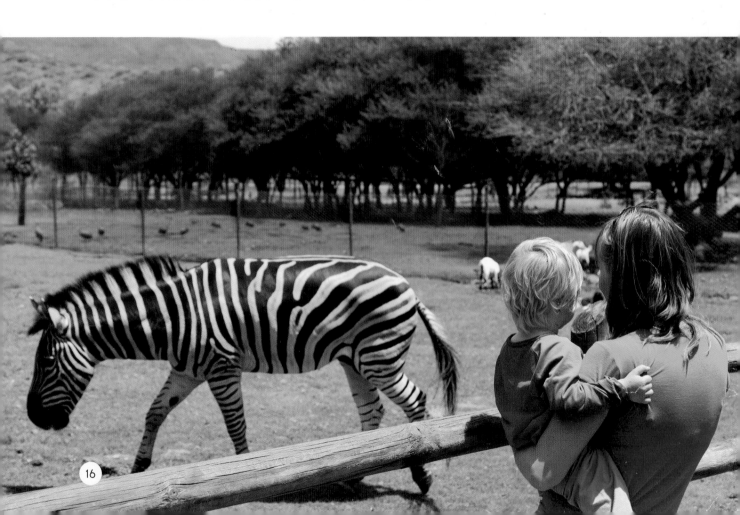